LISTEN IN 1

David Nunan

INTERNATIONAL
THOMSON
ASIA ELT

Thomson Asia Pte Ltd

Singapore • Albany • Belmont • Bonn • Cincinnati • Detroit • Johannesburg
London • Madrid • Melbourne • Mexico City • New York • Paris • Tokyo • Toronto

First published 1997 by:
International Thomson Asia ELT
60 Albert Street
#15-01 Albert Complex
Singapore 189969

The publication of *Listen In: Book One* was directed by the International Thomson Asia ELT Team:
- Karen Chiang, *Editorial Manager*
- Christopher Wenger, *Development Editor*
- Joan Quick, *Development Editor*
- Teri Tan, *Production Editor*
- Connie Wai, *Production Co-ordinator*

Designed by Raketshop Design Studio, Philippines:
- Leo Cultura, *Creative Director*
- Ibarra Crisostomo, *Book Designer*
- Glen Giron, *Illustrator*
- Eric Elayda & Donna Guerrero, *Computer Artists*
- Agnes Malinis & Luthy Pasamonte, *Copy Editors*

Printed by Chong Moh Offset Printing Pte Ltd, Singapore

1 2 3 4 5   01 00 99 98 97
ISBN 0-534-83536-8

AUTHOR'S ACKNOWLEDGEMENTS

First and foremost, I should like to acknowledge Karen Chiang, who first encouraged me to undertake this project, and who fully supported my desire to base the series on concepts of authenticity, task-based learning, and learner-centered instruction. Secondly, thanks are due to Chris Wenger, my editor, for his generous praise when I got it right, and his tactful guidance when I got it wrong. To Raketshop Design Studio, whose creativity and imagination are evident on every page, I can only say "thank you." Heartfelt thanks are also due to those friends and acquaintances who assisted in the collection of the authentic data that make this publication special. Last, but not least, thanks to Bob Cullen, without whose vision, energy and determination this series would not have happened.

In addition to the above, I would also like to thank the following professionals for their invaluable comments and suggestions during the development of this text:

KOREA
- David Bohlke, *Seoul City University*
- Cathy Rudnick, *Hanyang University*
- Patti Hedden, *Yonsei University*
- Jason Park, *Korea University of Foreign Studies*
- Michael Noonan, *Kook Min University*
- Mia Kim, *Kyunghee University*

TAIWAN
- Ann-Mare Hadzima, *National Taiwan University*
- Mary Ying-Hsiu Ku, *Taipei Municipal First Girl's High School*
- May Tang, *National Taiwan University*
- Ju-Ying Vinia Huang, *Tamkang University*
- Li-Te Li, *Tung Fang B & E Vocational High School*
- Yu-Chen Hso, *Soochow University*
- Grace Chao, *Soochow University*

JAPAN
- John Smith, *International Osaka Owada Koko*
- Holly Winber, *Senzoku Gakuen Fuzoku Koko*
- Monica Kamio, *AEON Amity*
- Shiona MacKenzie, *Gakushuin Boys' Senior High School*
- Kerry Read, *Blossom English Center*
- Rhona McCrae, *Freelance English Instructor*
- Inga Jelescheff, *Saguragaoka High School*

PHOTO CREDITS

The ELT Editorial Team of International Thomson Publishing Asia would like to thank the following embassies and tourists boards in Singapore for the use of their extensive photo libraries for *Listen In: Book One*. They are, in alphabetical order:

- Australian Tourist Commission...*p.19*
- British Tourist Authority...*p.26 and p.70*
- India Tourist Office...*p.12*
- Indonesia Tourist Promotions Office...*p.26*
- Japan Embassy (Cultural Section)...*p.19*
- Korea National Tourism Corporation...*p.12 and p.19*
- Malaysian Tourist Promotions Board...*p.26*
- Royal Netherlands Embassy...*p.70*
- Singapore Tourist Promotions Board...*p.30*

Special thanks to friends and colleagues of ITP Asia for sharing their photographs with us and for adding to the ITP Asia Photo Collection.

Contents

Scope and Sequence

Unit	Title	Topics	Goals	Sources	Pronunciation
1	How do you do?	· Greetings · Names · Personal information	· Identifying self · Understanding greeting and leave-taking	· Party conversation · Answering machine message	Number of syllables in words
2	This is my family.	· Families · Relationships	· Identifying members of the family	· Casual conversation	Contrast of /s/ and /z/
3	That's her over there.	· Physical description · Colors · Size	· Identifying people through physical description	· News report · Office conversation description	Contrast of question and statement intonation
4	What languages are you studying?	· Languages	· Identifying languages · Understanding preferences	· Interviews · School conversation	Syllable stress
5	Where are you from?	· Cities · Countries · Nationalities	· Identifying where people are from	· Conversation at convention	Contrast of /z/ and /zh/
1-5	Review				
6	This is where I live.	· Types of homes · Rooms	· Understanding descriptions of homes	· Telephone inquiry · Real estate ad · Casual conversation	Voiced/unvoiced *th*
7	Where can I find the sporting goods?	· Shopping · Department stores · Ordinal numbers	· Identifying locations in a store · Recognizing ordinal numbers in rapid speech	· Face-to-face inquiry · Store announcement	Ordinal numbers
8	What do you do?	· Occupations · Abilities	· Identifying abilities · Identifying preferences	· Telephone inquiry · Interview · Casual conversation	Question intonation
9	We're meeting in the conference room.	· Workplace · Office items	· Identifying where things are · Listening to requests	· Answering machine message · Workplace conversation · Face-to-face inquiry	Unstressed /ə/
10	Do you have a computer?	· Leisure · Electronic entertainment	· Identifying preferences	· News broadcast · Interview	Syllable stress
6-10	Review				

Unit	Title	Topics	Goals	Sources	Pronunciation
11	I usually get up at at six.	· Daily routines · Time	· Identifying times and schedules	· Monolog · Announcement	Reduced form of *do*
12	I'd like a table for five.	· Restaurants · Food	· Understanding requests · Confirming reservations	· Restaurant conversation · Telephone inquiry	Reduced form of *would, will*
13	Tennis is a great game.	· Sports	· Identifying sports · Understanding sports commentaries	· News report · Sports commentary	Word stress
14	What movies are playing?	· Entertainment	· Identifying invitations · Identifying types of entertainment	· Recorded announcement · Monolog	Question intonation
15	Where do you get your news?	· News · Weather · Money	· Identifying types of weather · Understanding news items	· News and weather reports	Word stress
11-15	Review				
16	I didn't know how to meet anyone.	· Meeting people	· Understanding a personal narrative · Identifying people through description	· Interview · Monolog	Identifying /or/ sound
17	Why don't we buy a new car?	· Plans · Suggestions	· Identifying and confirming intentions · Understanding excuses	· Casual conversation	Intonation to show surprise
18	My new boss is really nice.	· Personal traits and qualities	· Identifying personal qualities	· Casual conversation · Workplace conversation	Minimal pairs
19	How do you like to learn?	· Learning styles	· Identifying learning styles · Understanding questions	· Monolog · Oral test	Sentence rhythm
20	How often do you see your friends?	· Social networks	· Understanding surveys · Identifying social networks	· Survey · Casual conversation · Answering machine message	Contrast of /ay/ and /e/
16-20	Review				

How do you do?

GOAL
- Identifying self
- Understanding greeting and leave-taking

1 **What do people say when they meet for the first time?**
Check (✓) the boxes.

- ☐ How do you do?
- ☐ What are you doing?
- ☐ Hi, how's it going?
- ☐ Pleased to meet you.

- ☐ I'm going now.
- ☐ I'm John.
- ☐ This is Yumiko.
- ☐ What's the matter?

2 🔊 **Listen. How many voices do you hear? Circle a number.**

| 1 | 2 | 3 | 4 | 5 | 6 | 7 | 8 |

🔊 **Listen again and check (✓) the names you hear.**

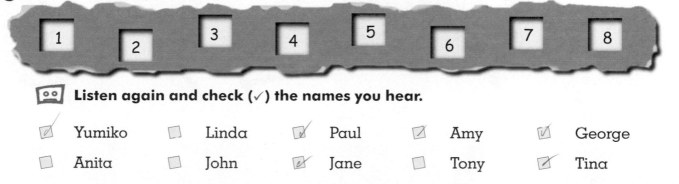

- ☑ Yumiko
- ☐ Linda
- ☑ Paul
- ☑ Amy
- ☑ George
- ☐ Anita
- ☐ John
- ☑ Jane
- ☐ Tony
- ☑ Tina

3 🔲 **Listen and check (✓) the names that have two syllables.**

☐ Lee	☑ Tony
☑ Yumiko	☑ Karen
☑ Sarah	☑ Kanittha
☐ Bob	☐ David
☑ Songporn	☐ Martha

🔲 **Listen and repeat.**

4 🔲 **Listen to the answering machine. Who can/can't come to Tony's party? Circle the correct answer.**

(Paul) can/can't come to the party.   John can/can't come to the party.

Yumiko can/can't come to the party.   Geoff can/can't come to the party.

Linda can/can't come to the party.   (Tina) can/can't come to the party.

🔲 **Listen again and check your answers.**
Now leave a message.

"Hi, Tony, this is _____. I'm calling to say I can/can't come to your party tonight."

5 Listen and check (✓) the names you hear.

- ✓ John Lee
- ✓ John Lowe
- ✓ Anita Tam
- ☐ Anita Lam
- ✓ Alan Walter
- ✓ Alan Walker

Listen again and check your answers.

6 Match each statement/question with the correct response.

a	Hello, Anita.	d	Hi, I'm Paul.
b	This is Alan Walker.	c	No, I'm John Lowe.
c	Are you John Lee?	b	Nice to meet you, Alan.
d	I'm Tony.	a	Hi, Yumiko.

Listen and check your answers.

7 🔊 **Listen and circle the right response for you.**

a ▶ Yes ✓ No   d ▶ Yes No ✓

b ▶ Yes No ✓   e ▶ Yes No ✓

c ▶ Yes ✓ No

8 **Write your name on a piece of paper and give it to the teacher. Take another piece of paper. Find the person.**

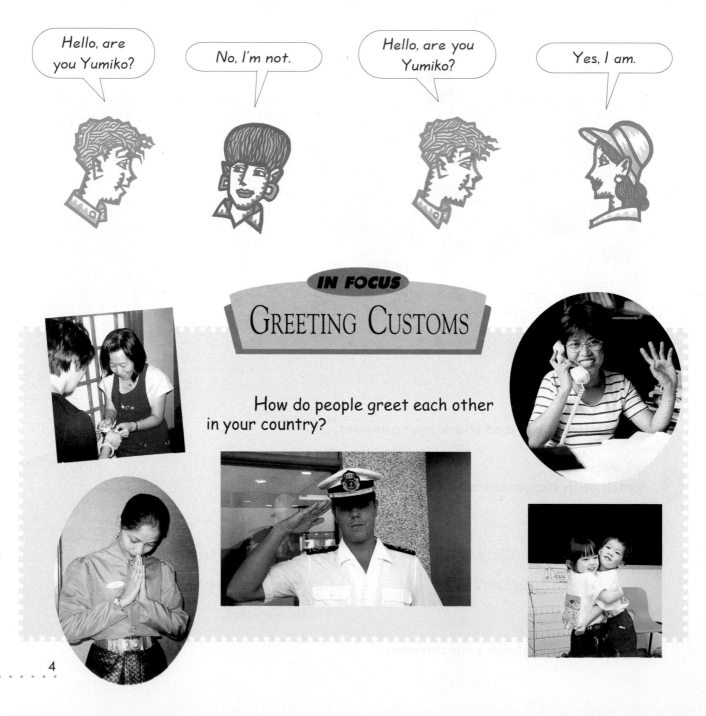

Hello, are you Yumiko?

No, I'm not.

Hello, are you Yumiko?

Yes, I am.

IN FOCUS

GREETING CUSTOMS

How do people greet each other in your country?

This is my family.

1 **Put the words in the correct box.**

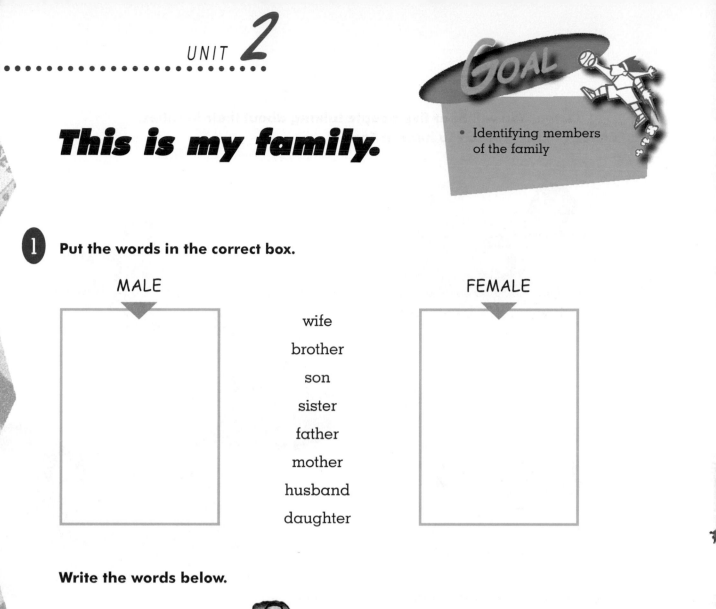

MALE

FEMALE

wife
brother
son
sister
father
mother
husband
daughter

Write the words below.

_____   _____   _____   _____

_____   _____   _____   _____

2 🔊 **Listen. You will hear five people talking about their families. Check (✓) the words you hear in Task 1.**

🔊 **Listen again and number the pictures.**

🔊 **Listen again. How many people can you find? Write the names you hear and check them with a partner.**

3 **Pair work. Imagine you are one of the people above. Describe your family. Your partner will guess which family is yours.**

This is my family. I have _____ sons / daughters / brothers / sisters, and _____ sons / daughters / brothers / sisters.

4 **Put the words in the correct column.**

/s/		/z/
aunts	:	sisters

sisters

aunts

brothers

parents

husbands

cousins

students

🔊 **Listen and check your answers.**

🔊 **Listen again and practice.**

5 🔊 **Listen to Tania and circle *True* or *False*.**

a	Tania is Canadian.	True	False
b	She is talking about her family.	True	False
c	She is going to Australia.	True	False
d	The daughter's name is Lisa.	True	False
e	The son's name is Tom.	True	False
f	Tania is nervous and excited.	True	False

🔊 **Listen again. Look at the picture and write the names.**

6 Listen and choose the right answer for you.

a ▷	Yes	No		d ▷	Yes	No
b ▷	Yes	No		e ▷	Yes	No
c ▷	Yes	No				

7 Pair work. Ask about your partner's family.

Do you have any brothers or sisters?

Yes, I have two brothers and a sister.

Tell another pair about your partner's family.

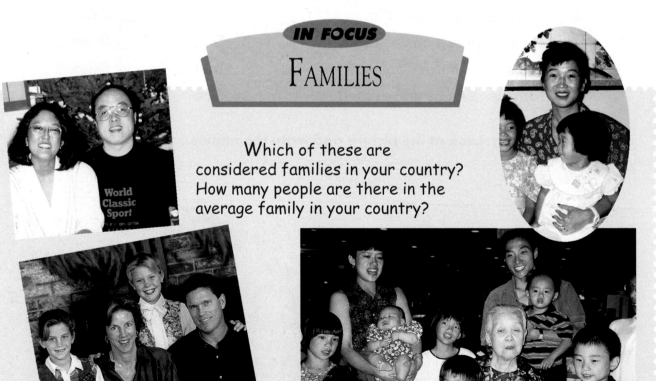

IN FOCUS

FAMILIES

Which of these are considered families in your country? How many people are there in the average family in your country?

That's her over there.

1 **Match the words with the correct group.**

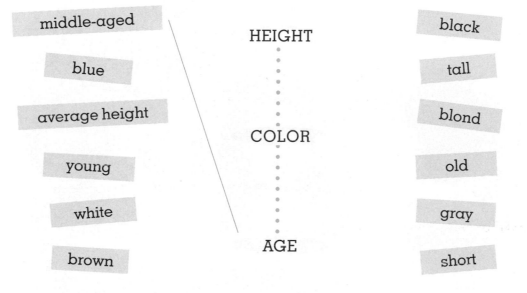

middle-aged

blue

average height

young

white

brown

HEIGHT

COLOR

AGE

black

tall

blond

old

gray

short

🔊 **Listen and circle the words you hear.**

2 🔊 **Listen. Who are the people describing? Circle the correct answer.**

Speaker 1	mother • daughter
Speaker 2	uncle • father
Speaker 3	sister • daughter
Speaker 4	friend • brother
Speaker 5	cousin • mother

Check your answers with a partner.

3 🔊 **Listen. You will hear two people talking about four of the people below. Write numbers (1–4) next to the people.**

4 **Pair work. Imagine you're one of the people above. Describe yourself. Your partner will guess who you are.**

Change roles and practice again.

5 🔊 **Is it a question or statement? Listen to the examples.**

EXAMPLE 1   He's the Managing Director? ↗   Question

EXAMPLE 2   He's the Managing Director. ↘   Statement

🔊 **Listen and circle the correct answer.**

a ▷	Question	Statement
b ▷	Question	Statement
c ▷	Question	Statement
d ▷	Question	Statement
e ▷	Question	Statement

6 🔊 **Listen and choose the right answer for you. Circle *Yes* or *No*.**

a ▷	Yes	No		d ▷	Yes	No
b ▷	Yes	No		e ▷	Yes	No
c ▷	Yes	No				

Pair work. Discuss your answers with a partner.

7 **Write a short description of yourself.**

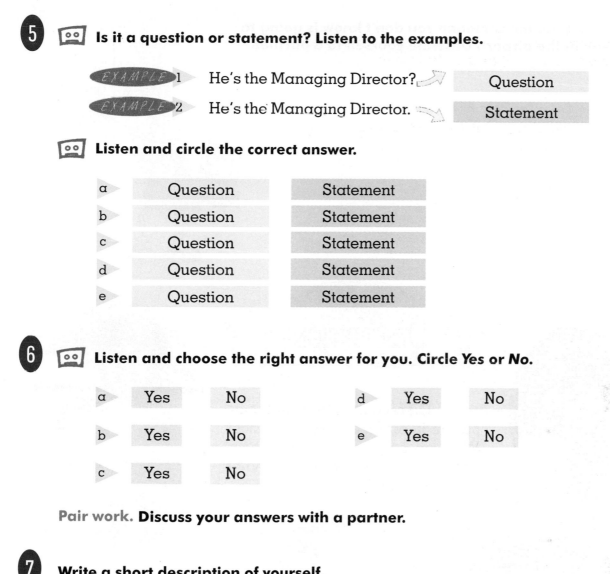

I'm cute!

Pair work. Imagine someone you don't know is going to meet you at the airport. Describe yourself to a partner.

I'm wearing a red shirt, my hair is blond, and well, I'm good-looking...

IN FOCUS

DESCRIPTIONS

Different cultures describe people in different ways. In most Western cultures, size, age, hair, and eye color are important. What is important in your culture?

What languages are you studying?

1 **Write the names of three countries where English is the *first* language, and three countries where it is a *foreign* language.**

Countries

First Language
1. _____
2. _____
3. _____

Countries

Foreign Language
1. _____
2. _____
3. _____

2 **Match the languages with the correct group.**

French   German
Korean   Thai
Spanish   Italian
Greek   Japanese
Indonesian   Hindi
Portuguese   Chinese

EUROPEAN   ASIAN

Listen. Which languages do you hear being spoken? Circle the answer.

a French / German

b Korean / Thai

c Portuguese / Greek

d Japanese / Indonesian

e Hindi / Chinese

Check your answers with a partner.

3 Pair work. **Look at the languages in Task 2. Where do people speak these languages? Make statements.**

People speak Portuguese in Portugal and Brazil.

4 **Listen to the conversation between an interviewer and a school counselor. What are they talking about?**

☐ The teaching of Asian languages
☐ The problem of teaching languages
☐ The different languages students can study

 Listen again and check (✓) the languages they talk about.

5 **Listen and underline the stressed syllable.**

Por•tu•guese   Chi•nese

Eng•lish   Ja•pa•nese

I•tal•ian   In•do•ne•sian

Ko•re•an

 Listen again and practice.

6 **Listen. Match the language with the name.**

French •
German •
English •
Korean •
Thai •
Spanish •
Japanese •
Chinese •

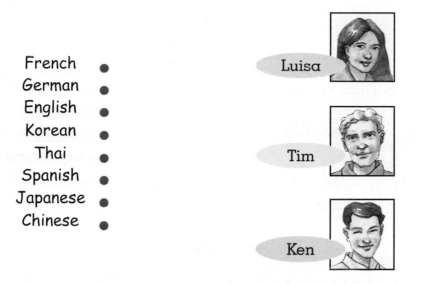

Luisa

Tim

Ken

 Listen again and make a note of why they are studying these languages.

Name

Reason

7 **Listen and circle the right response.**

a   At school.   Yes, I am.   d   Listening.   Yes, I do.

b   Three.   Yes, I do.   e   Japanese.   Yes, I do.

c   At school.   Yes, I do.

 Listen again and write the answers that are right for you.

a   _____   d   _____

b   _____   e   _____

c   _____

8 **Pair work. Discuss the questions with a partner.**

> 1   What languages are you studying? Why?
>
> 2   What other languages would you like to study? Why?

Talk about your partner with another student.

Yumi is studying English and Korean.

IN FOCUS

ENGLISH AROUND THE WORLD

Did you know that there are 36 countries in the world where English is spoken as a first language by a large number of people? How many countries can you name? Here are some of the countries where most of the population speaks English as a first language.

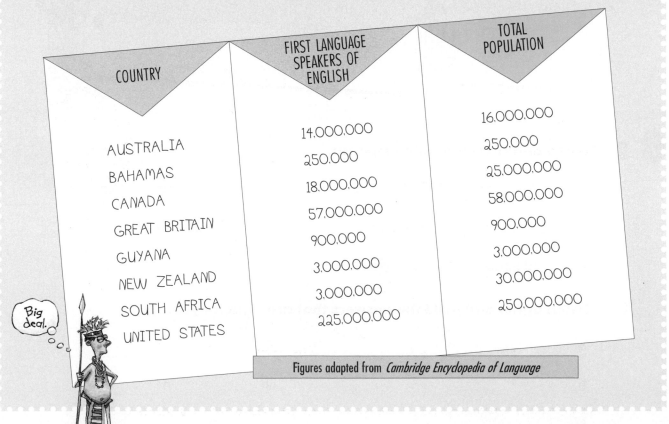

COUNTRY	FIRST LANGUAGE SPEAKERS OF ENGLISH	TOTAL POPULATION
AUSTRALIA	14,000,000	16,000,000
BAHAMAS	250,000	250,000
CANADA	18,000,000	25,000,000
GREAT BRITAIN	57,000,000	58,000,000
GUYANA	900,000	900,000
NEW ZEALAND	3,000,000	3,000,000
SOUTH AFRICA	3,000,000	30,000,000
UNITED STATES	225,000,000	250,000,000

Figures adapted from *Cambridge Encyclopedia of Language*

Big deal.

Where are you from?

1 **Match the cities and countries.**

Seoul	Japan
Bangkok	China
Shanghai	Korea
Taipei	Malaysia
Tokyo	Thailand
Kuala Lumpur	Taiwan

2 **Do you know where the places in Task 1 are? Write the cities on the map.**

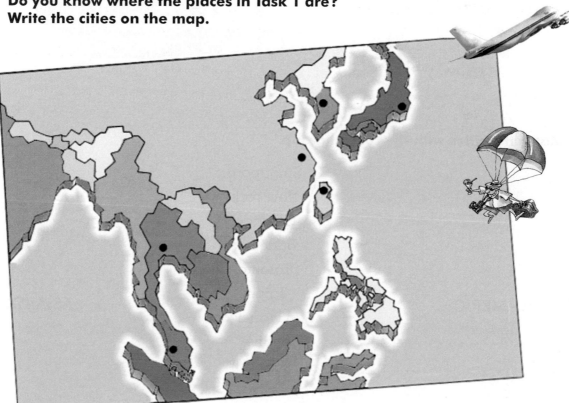

Check your answers with a partner. Can you think of any other cities in these countries?

3 Listen and number (1–3) the pictures.

4 Match the cities with the correct group.

Singapore
New York
Chicago
Bangkok
Toronto
Taipei
San Francisco
Sydney
Miami
Tokyo
Denver
Seoul

NORTH AMERICA

ASIA/PACIFIC

 Listen and circle the places you hear.

Listen again. Which cities do you think these words best describe?

beautiful _____

exciting _____

changing _____

large _____

5 🔊 **Listen. Which of the underlined sounds are the same?**
(Join the words with a line.)

| Malay<u>s</u>ian | Bra<u>z</u>ilian | A<u>s</u>ian | Chine<u>s</u>e |

🔊 **Listen again and practice.**

6 🔊 **Listen and choose the right answer for you.**

a ▸ Yes, I am.   No, I'm not.   d ▸ Yes, I am.   No, I'm not.

b ▸ Yes, I did.   No, I didn't.   e ▸ Yes, I do.   No, I don't.

c ▸ Yes, it is.   No, it isn't.

7 Write down three cities you would like to visit.

1. _____
2. _____
3. _____

Group work. Tell your partners.

> I would like to visit San Francisco, Shanghai, and Kyoto.

PEOPLE IN THE UNITED STATES

In the United States there are people from every corner of the world. The largest groups are Spanish speakers from Latin America. Other important groups are Chinese, Japanese, and Korean speakers from Asia. The largest groups from Europe are Germans and Italians.

What about your country? Are there people from other parts of the world? Where?

20

Review

1 🔊 **Listen and circle the names you hear.**

| Jane | Rick | Jim | Tina | Jenny |
| Michael | Rita | Nick | Rina | Dick |

🔊 **Listen again and number the pictures. One is not used.**

2 **Circle the word that does not belong.**

a ▷	Korea	Taipei	Manila	Singapore
b ▷	Mr.	Mrs.	Dr.	Ms.
c ▷	Professor	Kim	Hung	Koyama
d ▷	Chinese	Korean	Japanese	Taiwanese

3 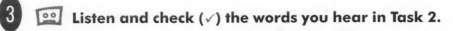 Listen and check (✓) the words you hear in Task 2.

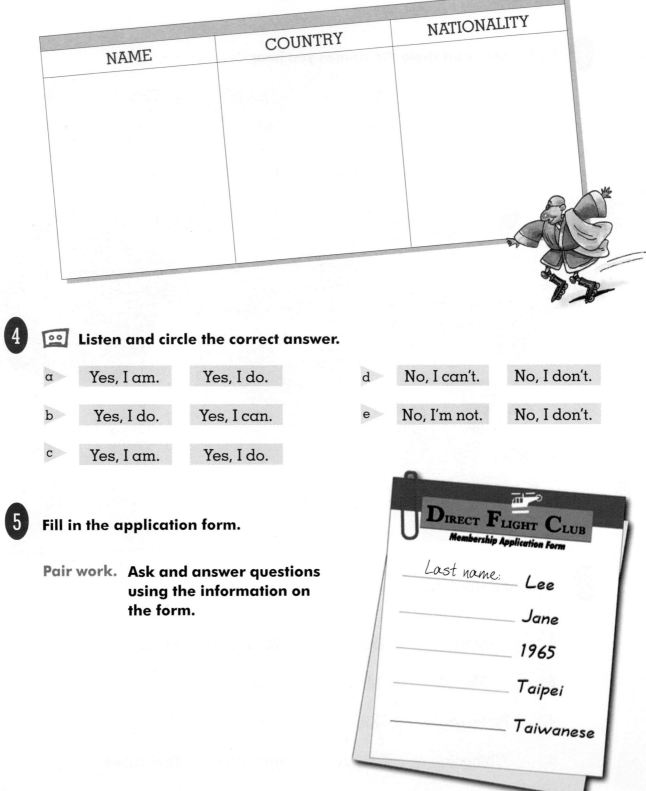

Listen again and fill in the attendance list.

NAME	COUNTRY	NATIONALITY

4 Listen and circle the correct answer.

a ▶ Yes, I am. Yes, I do. d ▶ No, I can't. No, I don't.

b ▶ Yes, I do. Yes, I can. e ▶ No, I'm not. No, I don't.

c ▶ Yes, I am. Yes, I do.

5 Fill in the application form.

Pair work. Ask and answer questions using the information on the form.

DIRECT FLIGHT CLUB
Membership Application Form

Last name: Lee

Jane

1965

Taipei

Taiwanese

This is where I live.

1 **Read the ads. How many times do these words appear?**

bedroom ___

bathroom ___

study ___

kitchen ___

balcony ___

FOR RENT

Lake Estates

Fully furnished, 4 bedrooms, 3.5 bathrooms, living and dining room, large kitchen, 3 fireplaces, and much more. Located next to Lake Hobart. Call 354-3819 for appointment.

Hilltop Real Estate

Truly unique! Professionally decorated, three bedrooms, two bathrooms. Kitchen recently remodeled. Balcony gives a great view of the city! Call for complete details.

Executive Towers

For professional. 2-bedroom condo near downtown business district. Kitchen/dining room, large study. Balcony overlooks river. 16th floor. Schedule a viewing today.

Homes Unlimited

Nice neighborhood. 3-bedroom house, 1 1/2 bathrooms, big family room, close to schools. Phone 383-1938 for more information.

Check your answers with a partner.

Can you find the names of any other parts of a home?

2 **Listen and check (✓) these words when you hear them.**

apartment	☐	rent	☐
neighborhood	☐	bedroom	☐
study	☐	living room	☐
dining room	☐	kitchen	☐
bathroom	☐	balcony	☐

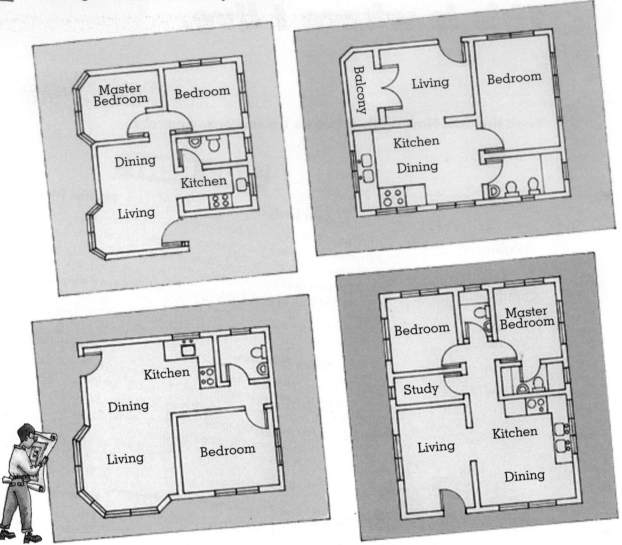

Listen again and find the apartment.

3 🔊 **Listen to the real estate ads. Are they for houses or apartments? Are the places for sale or rent? Circle the correct answers.**

a	House	Apartment	Sale	Rent
b	House	Apartment	Sale	Rent
c	House	Apartment	Sale	Rent

Check with a partner.
🔊 **Listen again to check your answers.**

4 🔊 **Listen and underline the words with the same sound as *th* in *there*. Circle the words with same sound as *th* in *three*.**

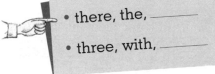

- <u>Th</u>ere are ⟨three⟩ apartments in <u>the</u> paper for rent.

- They said we can find our way with this map.

- Are these the things we need for the apartment?

Add another word to each list and practice.

- there, the, _____
- three, with, _____

5 🔊 **Listen and circle *True* or *False*.**

a	Haruko is talking to a real estate agent.	True	False
b	She is showing the other person some photographs.	True	False
c	She has rented a house.	True	False
d	The place is in Tokyo.	True	False
e	Her favorite room is the bedroom.	True	False

🔊 **Listen again and find Haruko's favorite room.**

6 🔈 **Listen and choose the right response.**

a	An apartment.	Yes, I do.
b	An apartment.	Yes, I do.
c	The study.	Yes, it is.
d	The study.	Yes, it is.
e	A balcony.	Yes, it does.

7 **Pair work. Describe one of the apartments in Task 2. Your partner will guess the one you're talking about.**

The apartment has _____ bedrooms. It has a _____ next to the _____ , and _____ is next to the _____ .

Change partners and practice again.

IN FOCUS

HOMES

Do you have traditional homes in your country? Do you know where these places are?

UNIT 7

Where can I find the sporting goods?

1 **Do you know these things? Match the name with the picture.**

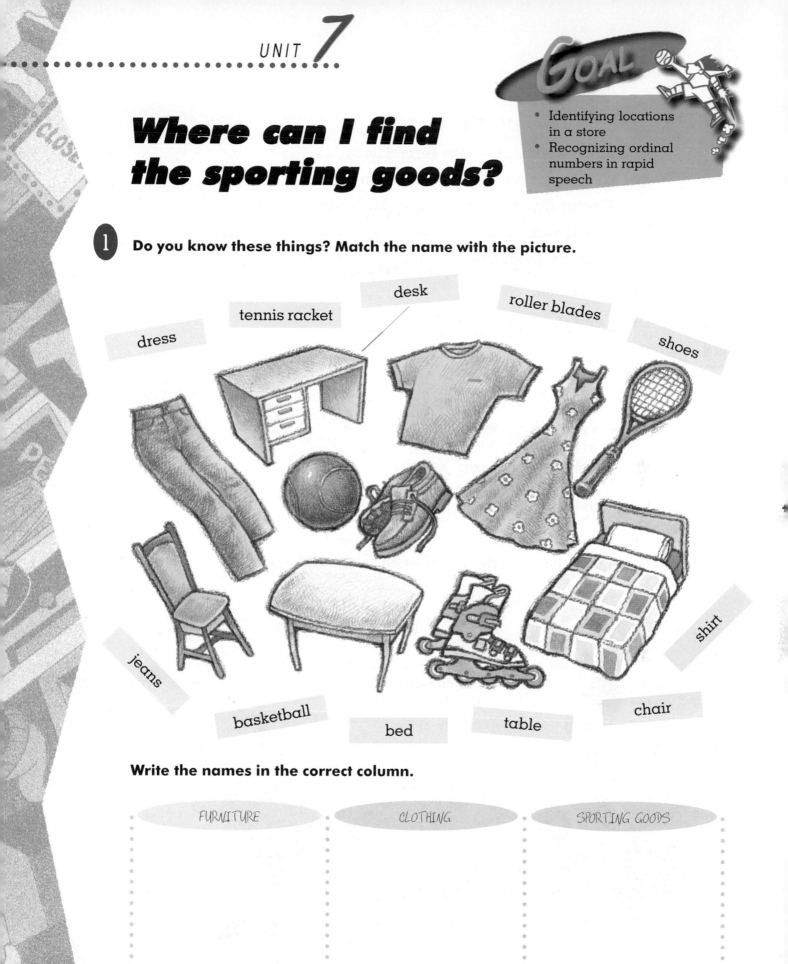

desk

tennis racket

roller blades

dress

shoes

jeans

basketball

bed

table

chair

shirt

Write the names in the correct column.

FURNITURE	CLOTHING	SPORTING GOODS

2 Write *in* or *on*.

a ► Men's wear is _____ the second floor.

b ► CD players are _____ the electrical goods department.

c ► Electrical goods are _____ the third floor.

d ► Tennis rackets are _____ the sporting goods department.

e ► Sporting goods are _____ the second floor.

Check with a partner.

 Listen and check your answers.

3 **Listen and circle the number you hear.**

a	second	seventh	d	first	fourth
b	first	fourth	e	second	seventh
c	fifth	sixth			

 Listen and practice.

4 **Listen and check (✓) the words when you hear them.**

children's wear ☐

travel goods ☐

electrical goods ☐

men's wear ☐

sporting goods ☐

women's wear ☐

restroom ☐

Listen again and label the places in Maxwell's.

Listen again.
Check (✓) the floors where there are special offers.

5 **Listen and look at the picture of the store. Circle the correct answer.**

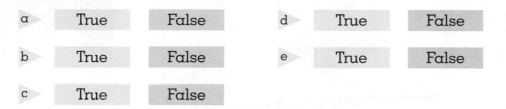

a ▸   True   False   d ▸   True   False

b ▸   True   False   e ▸   True   False

c ▸   True   False

6 Look at the shopping list and write the correct floors in Maxwell's.

Pair work. Take turns making statements about the store. Your partner will answer *true* or *false*.

SHOPPING LIST	FLOOR
necktie for Dad	_____
suitcase for trip to Europe	_____
T-shirt for Linda's baby	_____
skis for trip	_____
desk for my room	_____

IN FOCUS

DEPARTMENT STORES

Most countries have large department store chains. Japan has Mitsukoshi and Seibu. Robinson's is a large department store in Singapore. In the United States there is Macy's. Do you know the names of any other department stores in other countries? How many different "departments" can you name? Write the names and compare them with another student.

What do you do?

1 **Check (✓) the right columns for each occupation.**

	WORKPLACE		SALARY		
	indoors	outdoors	high	average	low
cook					
doctor					
gardener					
receptionist					
nurse					
singer					
waiter					
police officer					
computer operator					
salesclerk					

Pair work. Check your answers with a partner.

2 **Listen and number (1–4) the occupations you hear.**

3 🔊 **Listen to the responses and circle the right question.**

a ▶ What do you do?	• Where do you work?
b ▶ Can you use a computer?	• Do you use a computer?
c ▶ What do you look for in a job?	• Why do you want the job?
d ▶ How long have you been working?	• How long since you left school?
e ▶ Can you speak Japanese?	• Can you speak any other languages?

Check with a partner.
🔊 **Listen and check your answers.**

4 **What would you ask? Fill in the blanks.**

You want to know...	You ask...
EXAMPLE ... someone's occupation	What's your occupation?
a ... someone's phone number	_____
b ... someone's last job	_____
c ... where someone's from	_____
d ... someone's employer's name	_____
e ... what someone wants to be	_____

Where are you from?

I'm from San Francisco.

🔊 **Listen and check your answers.**

🔊 **Listen again and practice. Pay attention to the pronunciation of *your* and *you*.**

5 **Listen to the job interview. Circle the number of questions you hear.**

1   2   3   4   5   6

 Listen again. Circle *True* or *False*.

a ▷ Patricia can type.   True   False

b ▷ She can work nights.   True   False

c ▷ She can work Saturdays.   True   False

d ▷ She can speak another language.   True   False

e ▷ She can travel.   True   False

What job is Patricia interviewing for? Check (✓) the column.

yes   maybe   no

teacher

private secretary

nurse

salesclerk

singer

6 **Look at the occupations in Task 1.
Write three jobs you would like.**

Pair work. Tell a partner what you would like to be and why.

> Well, I'd like to be a singer.
> I like singing.

IN FOCUS

OCCUPATIONS

In the United States, men usually get the highest paying jobs. How about in your country? Who holds these jobs in your country?

Job (Ranked by salary)	Held mostly by
lawyer	men
airplane pilot	men
engineer	men
pharmacist	men
architect	men
teacher	women
plumber	men
social worker	women
cab driver	men
cashier	women

We're meeting in the conference room.

GOAL
- Identifying where things are
- Listening to requests

1 Circle the word that does not belong.

a	restroom	building	kitchen	conference room
b	left	right	on	straight ahead
c	receptionist	clerk	elevator	director
d	meeting	firm	discussion	chat

Check your answers with a partner.

2 🔲 **Listen to the answering machine and look at the words in Task 1. Check (✓) the words you hear.**

🔲 **Listen again and find the conference room.**

3 **Listen and match the pictures and conversations.**

Conversation _____   Conversation _____   Conversation _____

 Listen again. What are these people looking for?

1 _____   2 _____   3 _____

4 **Listen to the examples. Which underlined word is stressed? Check (✓) it.**

> EXAMPLE 1   "I need a computer <u>and</u> a calculator." ✓

> EXAMPLE 2   "I need a computer <u>and</u> a calculator."

 Listen and check (✓) the underlined words that are stressed.

a ▷ Well, the formatted disks <u>are</u> on the table.

b ▷ Well, I <u>can</u> add these figures up for you.

c ▷ I'll do them. I <u>can</u> add, you know.

d ▷ I need a computer <u>and</u> a calculator.

e ▷ The disks <u>are</u> on the table.

f ▷ I'm seeing the accountant at 1:00 <u>and</u> the manager at 2:00.

 Listen again and practice.

5 🔊 **Listen and circle the right answer for you.**

a ▷ | Yes, I do. | No, I don't. |

d ▷ | Yes, I do. | No, I don't. |

b ▷ | Yes, it is. | No, it isn't. |

e ▷ | Yes, I am. | No, I'm not. |

c ▷ | Yes, I do. | No, I don't. |

Pair work. Discuss your answers with a partner.

6 🔊 **Listen and draw lines to show where these things are.**

a ▷ scissors

d ▷ pencils

b ▷ computer paper

e ▷ computer disks

c ▷ address book

f ▷ memo pad

🔊 **Listen and circle *True* or *False*.**

a ▷ | True | False |

d ▷ | True | False |

b ▷ | True | False |

e ▷ | True | False |

c ▷ | True | False |

7 **Pair work. Practice asking and answering questions about the picture in Task 6.**

Practice asking about items in your classroom.

IN FOCUS

AT THE OFFICE

Compare the office of today
with the office of yesterday. How
many differences can you find?

Do you have a computer?

1 **Pair work. How many of the items can you name?**

What are these things used for? Check (✓) the columns.

	Education	Entertainment	Information
computer			
TV			
VCR			
video game system			
electronic diary			
stereo			
radio			

Pair work. Discuss your answers with a partner.

2 🔲 **Listen. Check (✓) the items in Task 1 that are mentioned in the news item.**

🔲 **Listen again and fill in the blanks.**

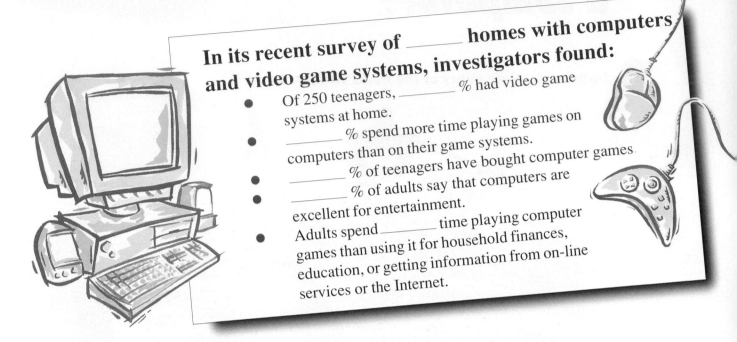

In its recent survey of _____ homes with computers and video game systems, investigators found:

- Of 250 teenagers, _____ % had video game systems at home.
- _____ % spend more time playing games on computers than on their game systems.
- _____ % of teenagers have bought computer games.
- _____ % of adults say that computers are excellent for entertainment.
- Adults spend _____ time playing computer games than using it for household finances, education, or getting information from on-line services or the Internet.

3 **Underline the words with three syllables. Then circle the words with the same stress as com-*pu*-ter.**

a ▸ Does the consumer favor Nintendo or Sega game systems?

b ▸ Are they intending to spend more on education or entertainment?

c ▸ Is the consumer demanding more interesting games these days?

d ▸ Are young people purchasing more video game systems than computers?

🔲 **Listen and check your answers.**

🔲 **Listen again and practice.**

4 **Tony, Lisa, and James are talking about using computers and video game systems.**
🔲 **Listen to the first part of the conversation and circle *True* or *False*.**

a ▸	Tony has a computer and a video game system.	True	False
b ▸	He uses the computer mainly for work.	True	False
c ▸	He spends more time on the computer.	True	False
d ▸	The game system is less fun.	True	False

Listen to the complete conversation and fill in the chart.

	Uses computers for	Spends more time using	More fun
TONY			
LISA			
JAMES			

5 **Listen and circle the right answer for you.**

a	Yes, I do.	No, I don't.	d	Yes, I do.	No, I don't.
b	Yes, I do.	No, I don't.	e	Yes, I do.	No, I don't.
c	Yes, I do.	No, I don't.			

Pair work. Discuss your answers with a partner.

6 **Which of the items do you have in your home? Which do you use?
Check (✓) the columns.**

	HAVE		USE	
	you	partner	you	partner
computer				
TV				
VCR				
video game system				
electronic diary				
stereo				
radio				

7 **Pair work. Ask a partner about the items in Task 6.**

Do you have a computer in your home?
Do you play video games?

Tell another pair about your partner.

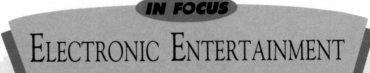

IN FOCUS
ELECTRONIC ENTERTAINMENT

Look at the following graphs. Do you think the information would be the same in your country?

What teenagers do on their computers

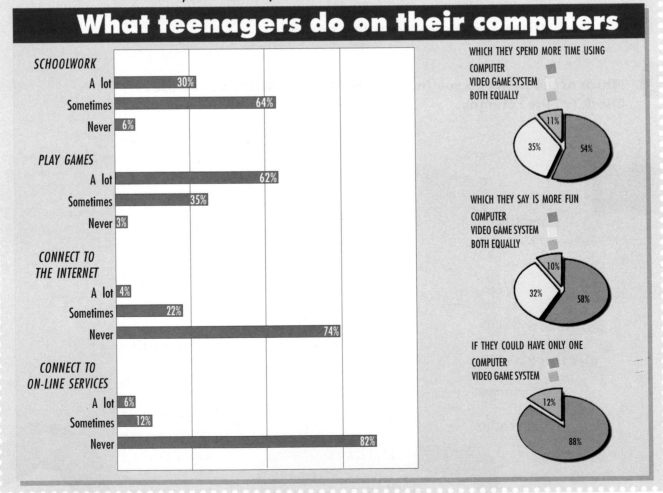

SCHOOLWORK
A lot 30%
Sometimes 64%
Never 6%

PLAY GAMES
A lot 62%
Sometimes 35%
Never 3%

CONNECT TO THE INTERNET
A lot 4%
Sometimes 22%
Never 74%

CONNECT TO ON-LINE SERVICES
A lot 6%
Sometimes 12%
Never 82%

WHICH THEY SPEND MORE TIME USING
COMPUTER
VIDEO GAME SYSTEM
BOTH EQUALLY
11% 35% 54%

WHICH THEY SAY IS MORE FUN
COMPUTER
VIDEO GAME SYSTEM
BOTH EQUALLY
10% 32% 58%

IF THEY COULD HAVE ONLY ONE
COMPUTER
VIDEO GAME SYSTEM
12% 88%

Review

1 Listen and check (✓) the names when you hear them.

Evelyn Kwok	Jason Lam	Alison Marianski
Janet Lai	Sonia Mason	Mr. Woo

Listen again and number the pictures (1–4).

2 Where would you use these things?
Check (✓) the columns.

	At Work			At Home		
	Yes	Maybe	No	Yes	Maybe	No
computer						
coffee machine						
fax machine						
answering machine						
color photocopier						
voice mail						
television						
video camera						
CD player						

Listen to the interview questions and check (✓) the words you hear.

Listen again and circle the right answer for you.

a	Yes, I can.	No, I can't.	d	Yes, I can.	No, I can't.
b	Yes, I do.	No, I don't.	e	Yes, I do.	No, I don't.
c	Yes, I have.	No, I haven't.			

3 Mr. Woo is talking to Alison. What equipment does he ask about? Listen and write the names you hear.

_____	Yes, I can.	No, I can't.
_____	Yes, I do.	No, I don't.
_____	Yes, I have.	No, I haven't.
_____	Yes, I can.	No, I can't.
_____	Yes, I do.	No, I don't.

Listen again. How does Alison respond? Circle the right answer. (NOTE: You won't hear the exact words.)

4 Listen and number the answers (1–5).

	Yes, I do.		I'm a receptionist.
	238 Fulton Drive		Smith, Lang and James
	Yes, I can.		

5 Pair work. Student A, you are an office manager and you are showing a new staff member around the office. Ask about five of the items in Task 2. Student B, you have just started work. Answer Student A's questions.

Can you use a computer?

Change roles and practice again.

I usually get up at six.

1 Match the pictures, activities, and times.

go to the gym

12:30 pm

have breakfast

6:00 am

go to bed

7:00 am

watch TV

11:00 pm

have dinner

7:00 pm

go to work

8:00 am

have lunch

5:30 pm

get up

8:30 pm

2 🔊 **Listen and number the times (1–6) when you hear them.**

3 🔊 **Listen to the questions and circle the best response.**

a   Oh, around eight thirty. • About noon.

b   At two thirty. • Twelve thirty every day.

c   Around six thirty, I guess. • Oh, around four.

d   Ten forty-five. • Seven o'clock.

e   Around seven thirty. • Usually around eleven.

4 🔊 **Agree or disagree? Listen to the examples.**

EXAMPLE 1   (Yes, it is.)   No, it isn't.

EXAMPLE 2   Yes, it is.   (No, it isn't.)

🔊 **Listen and circle the right response.**

a   Yes, it is.   No, it isn't.   d   Yes, it is.   No, it isn't.

b   Yes, it is.   No, it isn't.   e   Yes, it is.   No, it isn't.

c   Yes, it is.   No, it isn't.

5 🔊 **Listen and fill in the chart.**

PERSON	EVENT	TIME
Linda	gets up	8:00
	has lunch	4:00
	has dinner	8:15
Stella	leaves	11:00
	has lunch	6:00
	watches the news	10:00
		11:30
Sophie	goes to gym	3:30
	leaves home	7:00
	finishes work	11:30
	goes to bed	

🔊 **Listen again and find each person. Who do you think they are talking to?**

6 🔊 **Listen and choose the right answer for you.**

a ▸ True   False   d ▸ True   False

b ▸ True   False   e ▸ True   False

c ▸ True   False

7 🔊 **Questions like *When do you usually get up?* are often reduced.
Listen and repeat.**

🔊 **Listen and write the times that are correct for you.**

_____ Get up   _____ Come home

_____ Have breakfast   _____ Have dinner

_____ Go to school / work   _____ Watch TV, do homework

_____ Have lunch   _____ Go to bed

Pair work. Interview a partner about his/her daily routine.

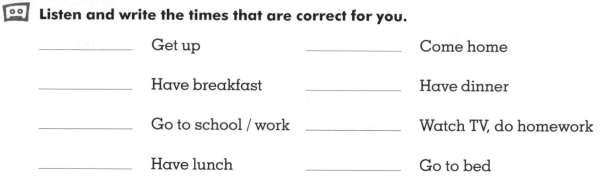

When do you
usually get up?

Around 7:30.

Tell another pair about your partner.

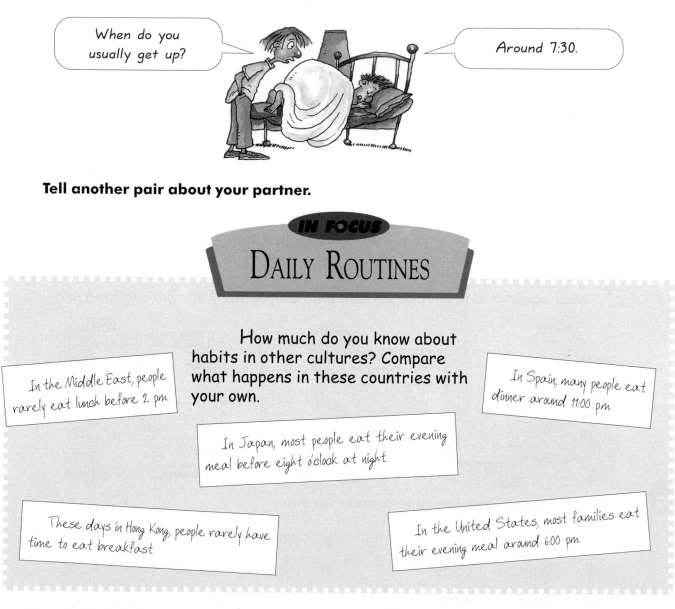

IN FOCUS

DAILY ROUTINES

How much do you know about
habits in other cultures? Compare
what happens in these countries with
your own.

In the Middle East, people
rarely eat lunch before 2 pm.

In Spain, many people eat
dinner around 11:00 pm.

In Japan, most people eat their evening
meal before eight o'clock at night.

These days in Hong Kong, people rarely have
time to eat breakfast.

In the United States, most families eat
their evening meal around 6:00 pm.

I'd like a table for five.

1 Write the words in the correct column.

Main Course	Dessert	Drink
_____	_____	_____
_____	_____	_____
_____	_____	_____
_____	_____	_____
_____	_____	_____
_____	_____	_____

steak
hamburger
salad
coffee
ice cream
fish
pasta
cake
tea
pizza
chicken
water

2 Listen. What are the people complaining about? Circle the correct item.

a   coffee   water

b   salad   ice cream

d   coffee   water

c   steak   cake

e   pasta   hamburger

3 🔊 **Listen. Which people are making *restaurant* reservations? Circle *Yes* or *No*.**

		Restaurant?		Successful?		
Conversation	1	Yes	No	Yes	No	Not sure
Conversation	2	Yes	No	Yes	No	Not sure
Conversation	3	Yes	No	Yes	No	Not sure
Conversation	4	Yes	No	Yes	No	Not sure
Conversation	5	Yes	No	Yes	No	Not sure

🔊 **Listen again. Which people *succeeded* in making a reservation? Circle *Yes*, *No*, or *Not sure*.**

4 🔊 **Listen and check (✓) if *would/will* is reduced.**

a ▷ _____ Would you like to see the menu?

b ▷ _____ Yes, I would.

c ▷ _____ I would like a hamburger.

d ▷ _____ What will you have to drink?

e ▷ _____ Will that be all?

🔊 **Listen and repeat.**

5 **Write *R* for people making reservations.**
Write *O* for people ordering food.

Did you want mustard on your hamburger?

Yes, please.

I'd like two seats for tomorrow night, please.

A table for five, please.

I'd like one medium pizza, please.

a ▷ _____   b ▷ _____   c ▷ _____   d ▷ _____

Check your answers with a partner.

Listen. How many people are ordering? Circle the number.

2   3   4   5   6

 Listen again and check (✓) the orders.

7 **Listen and circle the right response.**

a ▷ Yes, I am. • A hamburger, please.

b ▷ Yes, I am. • A hamburger, please.

c ▷ Yes, I would. • Medium rare, please.

d ▷ Yes, I would. • Medium rare, please.

e ▷ Yes, I did. • A coffee, please.

f ▷ Yes, I did. • A coffee, please.

8 **Pair work. Take turns being a waiter/waitress and a customer. Use the menu.**

Are you ready to order?

Yes, I'd like. . .

MENU

•••••••••• SOUP ••••••••••
Hot Shrimp Soup
French Onion Soup

•••••••••• SALAD ••••••••••
Caesar Salad
Macaroni Salad

•••••••••• MAIN DISH ••••••••••
Roast Chicken
Beef Stew
Pork Teriyaki

•••••••••• DESSERT ••••••••••
Choco Peanut Butter Mousse
Apple Pie
Mango Crepe

•••••••••• DRINKS ••••••••••
Pineapple Juice
Soda
Iced Tea

IN FOCUS
TABLE SETTINGS

Is there a traditional setting in your country? How is it similar to the one below? How is it different?

Do you know which to use? Write the number next to the correct item.

1 main course fork	3 soup spoon	5 salad fork
2 main course knife	4 coffee spoon	6 bread knife

Tennis is a great game.

1 Match the picture with the sport.

——— golf

swimming

tennis

running

ice hockey

soccer

basketball

skiing

2 Listen and check (✓) the sports you hear in Task 1.

3 Which words are stressed? Listen and underline them.

a ▶ Tennis is really great.

b ▶ Her father's a golf pro.

c ▶ Can you play badminton?

d ▶ I have tickets for the ball game.

e ▶ Who's the player on the left?

Listen again and practice.

4 Pair work. Match the word with the sport. Write the number.

1 ▶ swimming

2 ▶ tennis

3 ▶ soccer

field .... ▶ 3

set .... ▶

serve .... ▶

match .... ▶

goal .... ▶

water .... ▶

court .... ▶

umpires .... ▶

Check your answers with another pair.

5 🔲 Listen and answer *True* or *False*.

Commentary 1

This commentary is at a tennis match. T F

It is a match between two men. T F

It is very hot. T F

One of the players is called Jim Stone. T F

Commentary 2

This commentary is at a soccer match. T F

One side scores. T F

The game ends. T F

Commentary 3

This commentary is at a swimming competition. T F

It's an international competition. T F

The champion from Australia has won the race. T F

🔲 **Listen again and check your answers in Task 4.**

54

6 **Which sports can you play? Check (✓) the column.**

	You		Student 1		Student 2	
	can	can't	can	can't	can	can't
golf	——	——	——	——	——	——
running	——	——	——	——	——	——
ice hockey	——	——	——	——	——	——
tennis	——	——	——	——	——	——
soccer	——	——	——	——	——	——
basketball	——	——	——	——	——	——
skiing	——	——	——	——	——	——
swimming	——	——	——	——	——	——

Pair work. **Ask two other students and check (✓) their responses.**

Discuss the information with another student.

7 **How often do you do these things? Listen and circle the right answer for you.**

a	Often	Sometimes	Never
b	Often	Sometimes	Never
c	Often	Sometimes	Never
d	Often	Sometimes	Never
e	Often	Sometimes	Never

Group work. Discuss your answers with 3-4 other students. How healthy are you?

IN FOCUS

EVERYDAY ACTIVITIES

This is how people in the United States and Japan spend their time. What are the major differences between the two countries? How do you think they compare with your country? How do they compare with you?

	MINUTES / DAY	
	USA	**JAPAN**
Cook and eat meals	110	60
Do housework	75	70
Watch TV	160	50
Work	480	550
Talk to friends	90	60
Watch sports	20	20

What movies are playing?

1 Match the picture with the statement.

"Let's go dancing tonight."

"I have tickets for the new movie at the Odeon."

"Would you like to have dinner tonight?"

"This is a great computer game."

"Let's go to a concert."

2 **Listen. Which are invitations? Circle *Yes* or *No*.**

a	Yes	No	c	Yes	No	e	Yes	No
b	Yes	No	d	Yes	No			

 Listen again and check your answers.

3 🔊 **Listen. Do the questions have rising ⤴ or falling ⤵ intonation? Circle the correct answer.**

a	Rising	Falling	d	Rising	Falling
b	Rising	Falling	e	Rising	Falling
c	Rising	Falling	f	Rising	Falling

🔊 **Listen again and practice.**

4 **Note the types of entertainment. Write the number (1-4) next to the ads.**

Write the key words that gave you the clue.

Key Words

1. Music _____
2. Theater _____
3. Exhibition _____
4. Film _____

ENTERTAINMENT

☑2 **Shattered!** The award winning production by celebrated playwright Christopher Wenger, 7:30 pm Trocadero, Matinee 2 pm Sat. and Sun. Ticketing at all Urbtix. • • • • • •

☐ **Sydney Youth Orchestra.** 8 pm, San Francisco Civic Centre Admission by donation. • • • • • •

☐ Modern Sounds by South Asti Jazz Workshop. 8 pm. Foyer, Cultural Center. • • • • • •

☐ **The Gold Rush.** A series of paintings done of the Gold Rush of the 1880s. 10 am - 6 pm daily. Wagner Art Gallery, 4 Duddell Street. • • • • • •

☐ **Exploration Production.** Let's Hang Out: Presented by the Regional Council, a new play written by Terry Laine about troubled youth. May 4 - 10, Market Street Community Hall.

☐ **Focus at the Front Line.** A photo-journalistic account of 1996. 80 black and white photographs, jointly presented by the Arts Center and the San Francisco Press Photographers' Association 9 am - 10 pm daily, Arts Center, ends Sun.

☐ **Get Lofty** Prepare to go ballistic! Starring Jean Travolta. Majestic Cinema, North Beach. At 12:30, 2:30, 5:30, 7:30, 9:30, 11:30.

☐ **Contemporary Art from Seoul.** 9:30 am - 6 pm except Sundays and public holidays. Fung Pin Shan Gallery, Chinatown. Ends today.

5  **Listen to the announcement. How many different events do you hear?**

        3   4   5   6   7

Listen again and number (1-4) the ads in Task 4 when you hear them.

6 **Listen and circle the right response for you.**

    a   OK. • Sorry, I can't tonight.

    b   Yes, I would. • No, I wouldn't. Sorry.

    c   Great. I'd love to go. • I can't make it, I'm afraid.

    d   All right. • I'm not really interested in that sort of thing.

    e   Sounds great. • No, thanks.

Pair work. Discuss your answers with a partner. Give reasons.

7 **What do you do for entertainment? Make a list.**

Pair work. Discuss your list with a partner. Then practice making invitations.

Let's go to the play at the Trocadero.

IN FOCUS

LEISURE THROUGH THE AGES

Do you know when these forms of entertainment and leisure were popular? Are any still popular now? Check (✓) the column and then discuss your answers with a partner. Can you add any items to the list? What do you do in your leisure time?

	Twenty years ago	Fifty years ago	Now
Ballroom dancing	_____	_____	_____
Watching TV	_____	_____	_____
Storytelling	_____	_____	_____
Walking	_____	_____	_____
Watching movies	_____	_____	_____
Watching videos	_____	_____	_____
Going to coffee shops	_____	_____	_____
Going on drives	_____	_____	_____
Going to dinner parties	_____	_____	_____

Where do you get your news?

- Identifying types of weather
- Understanding news items

1 Do you know these words? Which words describe the weather where you live? Check (✓) the column.

	January	July
hot	_____	_____
humid	_____	_____
cold	_____	_____
cool	_____	_____
mild	_____	_____
rainy	_____	_____
fine	_____	_____
snowy	_____	_____
	_____	_____

2 🔲 Listen. Is the report about news or weather? Check (✓) the column.

	News	Weather	Key Words
Seoul	_____	_____	_____
Bangkok	_____	_____	_____
Taipei	_____	_____	_____
Osaka	_____	_____	_____
Kuala Lumpur	_____	_____	_____
Jakarta	_____	_____	_____

🔲 Listen again. Write the key words that gave you the clue. Check your answers with a partner.

3 **Listen and check (✓) the countries you hear.**

Listen again. Which countries use *dollars?* Check (✓) Yes or No.

		Yes	No
United States	_____	_____	_____
Japan	_____	_____	_____
Singapore	_____	_____	_____
Thailand	_____	_____	_____
New Zealand	_____	_____	_____
Korea	_____	_____	_____
Malaysia	_____	_____	_____
Australia	_____	_____	_____

Listen again and fill in the exchange rates.

US$1.00 = _____ Japanese yen

US$1.00 = _____ Singapore dollars

US$1.00 = _____ Australian dollars

US$1.00 = _____ Korean won

US$1.00 = _____ New Zealand dollars

4 🔊 **Listen to the examples. Which is more important, *what* happened or *when* it happened?**

	WHAT	WHEN
EXAMPLE 1	✓	
EXAMPLE 2		✓

🔊 **Listen and check (✓) the correct column.**

	WHAT	WHEN
a		
b		
c		
d		
e		
f		

5 🔊 **Listen to the weather forecast and circle the numbers you hear.**

18	19	20	21	22	23
24	25	26	27	28	29

🔊 **Listen again and check (✓) the words you hear in Task 1.**

🔊 **Now listen and write the temperatures in the chart.**

WEATHER REPORT	
Bangkok	
Beijing	
Tokyo	
Hong Kong	
Seoul	

6 🔊 **Listen to the weather forecasts again. Where might you need these things? Write the name of the city.**

_____ _____ _____ _____ _____ _____

Pair work. Discuss your answers with a partner.

a	always	often	sometimes	hardly ever	never
b	always	often	sometimes	hardly ever	never
c	always	often	sometimes	hardly ever	never
d	always	often	sometimes	hardly ever	never
e	always	often	sometimes	hardly ever	never

8 **Pair work. Make up a weather forecast for your city today. Report your forecast to the class.**

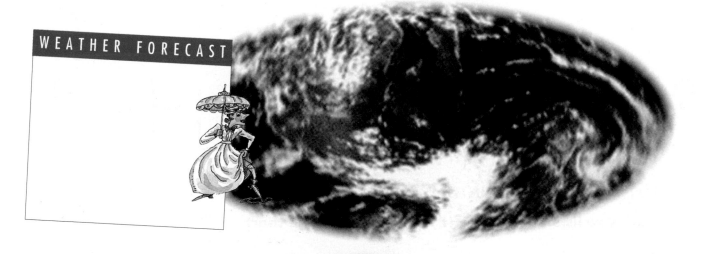

WEATHER FORECAST

IN FOCUS

NEWS SOURCES

In a recent survey, people said that they get news from the following sources. Check (✓) where you get your news. Discuss your answers with a partner.

	Usually	Sometimes	Never
TV	_____	_____	_____
Radio	_____	_____	_____
Newspapers	_____	_____	_____
Magazines	_____	_____	_____
The Internet	_____	_____	_____
Other people	_____	_____	_____

Review

1 🔊 **Listen and check (✓) the times you hear.**

🔊 **Listen again. Match the clock with the picture.**

2 **Check (✓) the words that describe temperature.**
Underline the words that describe weather you like.

☐ cold	☐ rainy	☐ cool	☐ humid
☐ windy	☐ mild	☐ hot	☐ freezing

🔊 **Listen and circle the words you hear.**

3 🔊 **Listen and write Joe and Jenny's order.**

The BRASSERIE

Chef Salad

_____

_____

_____

_____

_____

🔊 **Listen again. Write the other food words you hear.** 👉

_____

_____

4 **How do you spend your leisure time?**
🔊 **Listen and circle the right response for you.**

S					
U	a	Often	Sometimes	Hardly ever	Never
R	b	Often	Sometimes	Hardly ever	Never
V	c	Often	Sometimes	Hardly ever	Never
E	d	Often	Sometimes	Hardly ever	Never
Y	e	Often	Sometimes	Hardly ever	Never

Group work. Discuss your answers.
Which activity is the most popular in your class?

5 **Write down your schedule for tomorrow on a piece of paper. Don't write your name.**

Give the schedule to your teacher.
Take another schedule.
Ask questions to find out whose schedule you have.

7:00 – Tennis Lesson
8:00 – breakfast with Joe
8:45 – Leave for office
12:00 – Lunch

I didn't know how to meet anyone.

GOAL

- Understanding a personal narrative
- Identifying people through description

1 **Where do you think people meet new friends? Write numbers in the spaces.**

1 ▷	This is a common way for people to meet.
2 ▷	This is rather unusual.
3 ▷	This is extremely unusual.

☐ ◁ at school

☐ ◁ at work

☐ ◁ at a shopping mall

☐ ◁ through an introduction agency

☐ ◁ at a party

☐ ◁ through a friend or relative

☐ ◁ at a sports club

Group work. Discuss your answers. Which do you think is the most *common* way for people to meet? Which is the most *unusual* way?

2 🔊 **Listen and fill in the chart.**

PERSON	BEST FRIEND	HOW MET?
Liz Charlotte Chuck		

3 🔊 **Listen and circle the right response.**

a ▷ Yes, she is. • Samantha.

b ▷ Yes, I did. • Tony.

c ▷ No, she isn't. • Martina.

d ▷ No, he isn't. • Chuck.

e ▷ Yes, I did. • At my brother's place.

Check with a partner.

🔊 **Listen again and check your answers.**

4 🔊 **Listen to the people describing themselves on an introduction agency tape. Write the names next to the correct information.**

works at home _____

rather short _____

wants a tennis partner _____

likes to travel _____

works in a school _____

likes to have fun _____

likes to talk _____

plans to be a doctor _____

🔊 **Listen again and find each person. Write the name.**

5 Pair work. **Who is the most interesting/least interesting person in Task 4? Give reasons. Discuss your choices with another pair.**

I think _____ is the most interesting because...

6 Listen and number (1–8) the information in the correct order.

Information

- Likes
- Height
- Name
- Where he works
- Eyes
- Wants to meet
- Where he lives
- Hair

Make up your own introduction. Read your introduction to 3–4 other students.

7 **Imagine someone is calling from an introduction agency.** Listen and circle the right response for you.

a ▶ Yes, I am. • I guess I'm kind of average. • Not really.

b ▶ Oh, all the time. • Now and then. • No, I don't, I'm afraid.

c ▶ Yes, I do. • No, I don't.

d ▶ Yes, I love them. • I don't mind them. • No, I don't.

e ▶ Doesn't everyone? • Occasionally. • No, I prefer a quiet time.

8 Which word in each group has the same sound as **o** in **or**? Circle it.

a ▶	**hot**	short	long	blond
b ▶	**four**	boys	Mom	brown
c ▶	**two**	do	both	door
d ▶	**does**	choose	your	brother

🔊 **Listen and check your answers.**

🔊 **Listen again and practice.**

IN FOCUS

SURVEY

A survey in the United States showed that most people met their partners through other friends. Other popular ways for people to meet were through work, at parties, and through leisure and sporting activities. How do people meet in your country?

Group work. Conduct a class survey. How did most people meet their best friend? Which is the most common way? Which is the most unusual way?

Why don't we buy a new car?

1 How often do you plan the following with your family or friends? Check (✓) the column.

	Regularly	Sometimes	Rarely	Never
buying a car				
buying furniture				
going on vacation				
how to spend the weekend				
organizing a party				

2 📟 Listen and number (1-3) the pictures.

3 Match the suggestion with the objection.

a	Let's go see the new movie.	I can't play.
b	Why don't we buy a new car?	It's too cold.
c	How about a game of tennis?	I've seen it.
d	Let's go to the beach.	He's out of town right now.
e	Why don't we visit your brother?	We can't afford it.

🔊 **Listen. Do the objections have the same meaning as the ones above? Circle *Same* or *Different*.**

a ▶ Same   Different   d ▶ Same   Different

b ▶ Same   Different   e ▶ Same   Different

c ▶ Same   Different

4 Write a number (1-3) to show what people are doing.

Are they...

1. making a suggestion?
2. expressing an objection?
3. agreeing with a suggestion?

_____ It's too cold.

_____ That's a great idea.

_____ Let's go to the ball game tomorrow night.

_____ I'm out of cash right now.

_____ How about inviting the Browns over?

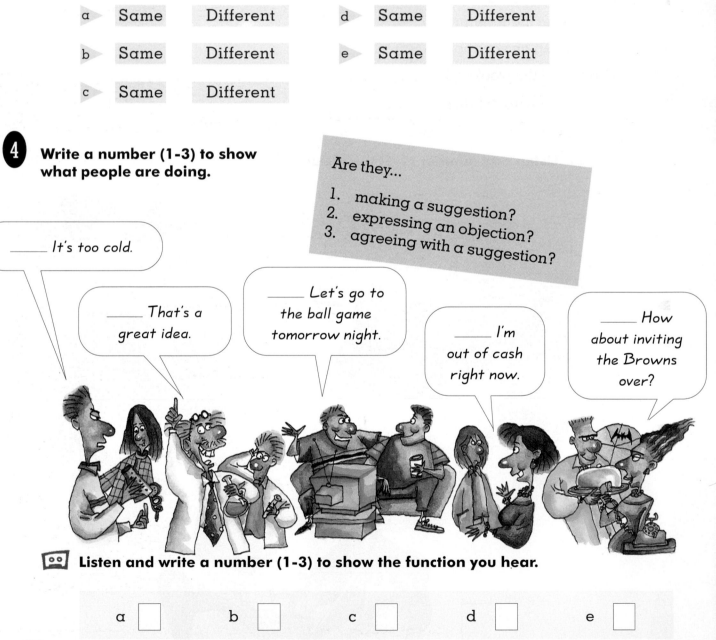

🔊 **Listen and write a number (1-3) to show the function you hear.**

a ☐   b ☐   c ☐   d ☐   e ☐

5 🔲 **Listen and check (✓) the responses that show *surprise*.**

a ▸ _____ You can't, huh? That's too bad.

b ▸ _____ You are? But you promised.

c ▸ _____ You did? That's great.

d ▸ _____ I can't. I have to work.

e ▸ _____ You did? Then what are we going to serve the guests?

🔲 **Listen again and practice.**

6 🔲 **Listen to Tom and Sally planning their weekend. How many suggestions does Sally make? Circle the number.**

1 2 3 4 5 6

🔲 **Listen again and fill in the blanks.**

Suggestion ▼	Objection ▼
	It might rain.
_____	
See the new movie at the Odeon.	_____
_____	Short of money.
Visit Tom's brother.	

What does Sally finally decide to do?

7 🔊 **Listen and check (✓) the right response for you.**

     a ▷   That's a good idea. • Oh, I'd rather not.

     b ▷   OK. • No, thanks.

     c ▷   Great! • No, thanks.

     d ▷   All right. • I have something else to do.

     e ▷   That's a great idea. • No, I'd rather stay home.

8   **Pair work. Take turns making suggestions and excuses.**

How about studying together after class?

Sorry, I have to go shopping with my sister.

IN FOCUS

MAKING EXCUSES

In some countries, it's okay to accept an invitation and then not show up. How about in your country? In most English-speaking countries, you should give a reason why you can't go.

I'm sorry I can't come to your party. I was really looking forward to it. I have to visit my sick aunt in the hospital.

My new boss is really nice.

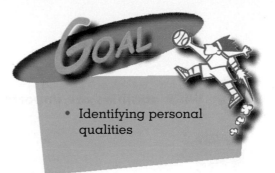

• Identifying personal qualities

1 Check (✓) the words you know. Look up the others in a dictionary. Put them in the correct column.

		Positive	Negative	Neutral
noisy	serious	_____	_____	_____
friendly	nervous	_____	_____	_____
interesting	boring	_____	_____	_____
stupid	calm	_____	_____	_____
lazy	smart	_____	_____	_____
nice	mean	_____	_____	_____
funny	hardworking	_____	_____	_____
confident	nasty	_____	_____	_____

Pair work. Discuss your answers with a partner.

2 🔊 Listen and write the words that describe each person.

Description	Opposite
_____	_____
_____	_____ 2.
_____	_____
_____	_____ 4.
_____	_____
_____	_____ 6.

Write the opposite of the words in Task 1.

3 **What qualities are important for these jobs? Write as many words as you like.**

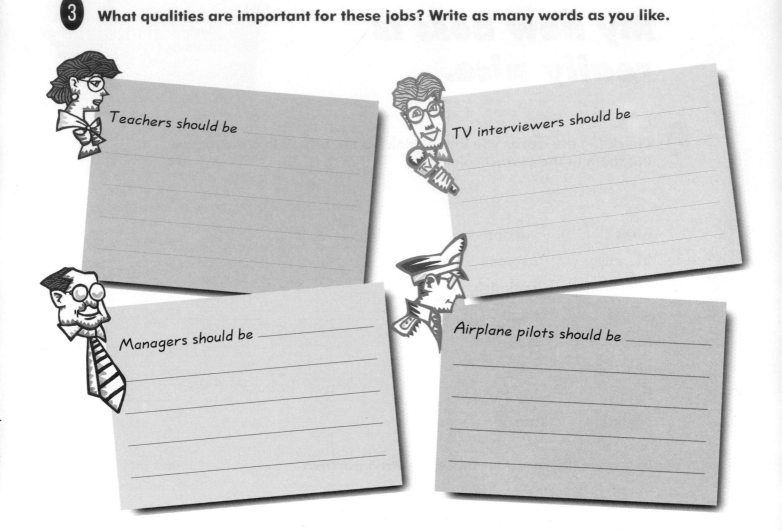

Teachers should be _____

TV interviewers should be _____

Managers should be _____

Airplane pilots should be _____

Pair work. Discuss your answers with a partner.

4 **Listen and check (✓) the word you hear first in each conversation.**

a ▷ ☐ quite   ☐ quiet

b ▷ ☐ live   ☐ leave

c ▷ ☐ brought   ☐ bought

d ▷ ☐ guess   ☐ guest

e ▷ ☐ sick   ☐ six

Listen and practice.

5 🔊 **Listen and number (1–5) the best response.**

☐ Yes, it is.

☐ Well, she's obviously very nice.

☐ Someone who's friendly.

☐ Yes, she is.

☐ That's true.

6 🔊 **Listen. Two people are discussing three applicants for a job. What do they say about each person?**

APPLICANT	QUALITIES
Julie Mendoza	_____
	_____
Rick Lamb	_____
	_____
Sally Crocker	_____
	_____

🔊 **Listen again. What do you think the job is?**

Pair work. Choose the best person for the job. Discuss your choice with another pair.

7 🔊 **Imagine you are having an interview. Listen and circle the right response for you.**

a ▸	Yes, I am.	Sort of.	Not really.
b	Yes, I am.	Sort of.	Not really.
c	Yes, I am.	Sort of.	Not really.
d	Yes, I do.	It's OK sometimes.	No, I don't.
e	Yes, I do.	No, I don't.	

8 **Pair work. Describe yourself to a partner.**

Well, I'm quiet, and rather serious. And I . . .

IN FOCUS

PERSONALITY

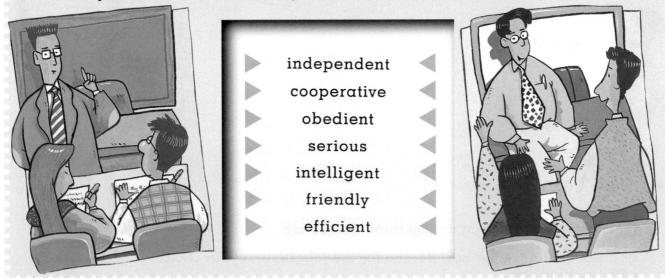

Personality qualities seem to be viewed differently in different cultures. In the United States, people view qualities such as independence and friendliness as good qualities. How about in your country? Which qualities do people think are best? Select two adjectives from the following list and discuss them with a partner.

▸ independent ◂
▸ cooperative ◂
▸ obedient ◂
▸ serious ◂
▸ intelligent ◂
▸ friendly ◂
▸ efficient ◂

How do you like to learn?

1 **Match each line with the correct ending.**

There are three basic types of learners:

a | Hearing learners learn best by | touching and doing things while learning.

b | Visual learners learn best by | listening to spoken language.

c | Tactile learners learn best by | reading or looking at pictures.

[00] **Listen and check your answers.**

2 [00] **Listen and circle the right answer for you.**

a ▷ Only one. • Two. • More than two.

b ▷ When I was a child. • In high school. • After high school

c ▷ I prefer listening. • I prefer reading.

d ▷ Speaking, definitely. • Writing.

e ▷ By myself. • With others.

3 🔊 **Anna is answering questions to find out her learning style. Listen and check (✓) the questions. (NOTE: They may not be the exact words.)**

⬭ QUESTIONS ⬭	⬭ ANSWERS ⬭
_____ Have you done this kind of test before?	_____
_____ How do you learn how a computer works?	_____
_____ How do you solve problems?	_____
_____ What's the last book you read for fun?	_____
_____ What do you do when you're not sure how to spell a word?	_____
_____ How do you study for a test?	_____
_____ What do you do when you're happy?	_____
_____ What do you think of when you hear the word C-A-T?	_____
_____ What kind of class did you like best?	_____
_____ How do you like to tell a story?	_____

🔊 **Listen again and make a note of Anna's answers.**

Pair work. What do you think? What kind of learner is Anna?

 ☐ hearing   ☐ visual   ☐ tactile

4 🔊 **Which sentences have the same stress as the example? Listen and underline the stressed syllables in each sentence.**

You learn to speak by speaking.

a   They learned to read by reading.

b   I like to learn by touching.

c   I used to learn Chinese.

d   She studied Japanese in school.

e   I read the book in English.

Check your answers with a partner.
🔊 **Listen again and practice.**

5 **Listen and circle the right answer for you.**

	a	Watch a video about it.
1	b	Get someone to explain it.
	c	Figure it out for myself.

	a	A book with lots of pictures.
2	b	A novel.
	c	A book with questions and puzzles.

	a	Write it down to see if it looks right.
3	b	Sound it out.
	c	Use a dictionary.

	a	Read a book.
4	b	Get someone to ask me questions.
	c	Make notes.

	a	Think of a picture of a cat.
5	b	Say the word *cat* to myself.
	c	Imagine being with a cat.

	a	An art class.
6	b	A music class.
	c	An exercise/aerobics class.

	a	Write it out.
7	b	Say it.
	c	Act it out.

Pair work. What type of a learner are you? Discuss your answers with a partner. Give reasons.

hearing ☐   visual ☐   tactile ☐

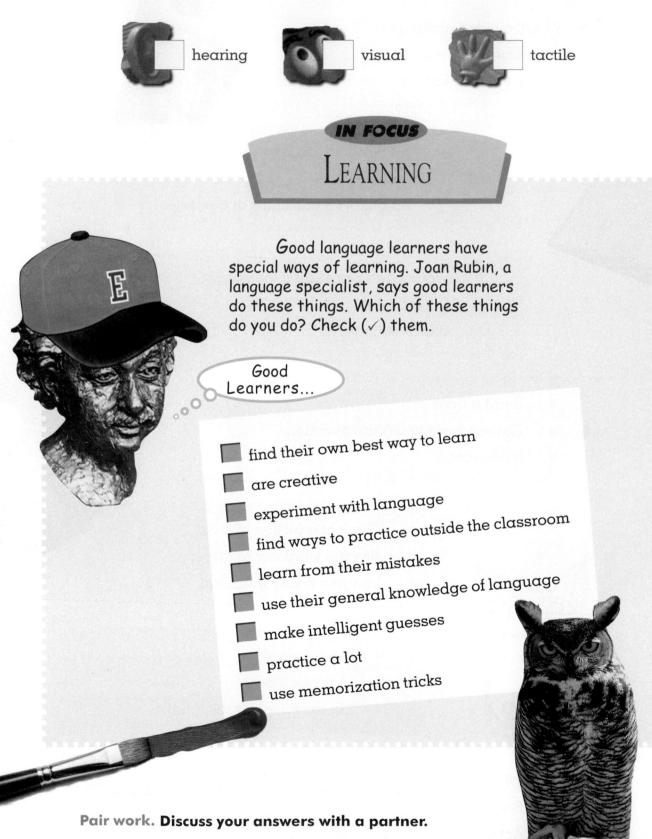

IN FOCUS

LEARNING

Good language learners have special ways of learning. Joan Rubin, a language specialist, says good learners do these things. Which of these things do you do? Check (✓) them.

Good
Learners...

☐ find their own best way to learn

☐ are creative

☐ experiment with language

☐ find ways to practice outside the classroom

☐ learn from their mistakes

☐ use their general knowledge of language

☐ make intelligent guesses

☐ practice a lot

☐ use memorization tricks

Pair work. Discuss your answers with a partner.

How often do you see your friends?

GOAL
- Understanding surveys
- Identifying social networks

1 **How often do you see these people? Check (✓) the right column for you.**

	Every day	Often	Every month	Hardly ever	Never
parent(s)					
brother(s)/sister(s)					
husband/wife					
best friend					
co-workers					
doctor					
mail carrier					

Pair work. Discuss your answers with a partner.

2 **Listen. These people are answering a survey. Who do they see every day? Check (✓) the correct answers.**

parent(s)				
brother(s)/sister(s)				
husband/wife				
children				
best friend				
other friends				
teacher				
co-workers/classmates				
boss				
secretary				

Listen again. Do they see other people not on the list? Write them.

others				

3 **Listen and circle the right answer for you.**

     a ▷ Sure. • Oh, well, I guess so.

     b ▷ Yes, I do. • Most days, I guess. • Well, not every day.

     c ▷ Of course. • Yes, almost every day. • No, I don't.

     d ▷ Yes, I do. • Yes, most days. • No, not every day.

     e ▷ Certainly. • Yes, usually. • No, I don't.

     f ▷ That's OK. • You're welcome.

Pair work. Discuss your answers with a partner.

4 **Listen and put the words in the correct column.**

| day | let's | May | neighbor | friend | letter | eight | station | mail | met | center |

/ay/	/e/
day	let's

 Listen again and practice.

84

5 🔊 **Listen. Who did the people talk to today?**

Zena _____

_____

Pete _____

_____

Rita _____

_____

David _____

_____

🔊 **Listen again and match the picture with the person.**

6 🔊 **Listen to the conversations in Task 5 again. Which topics do they discuss? Check (✓) the column.**

	Yes	No	Not sure
money	_____	_____	_____
movies	_____	_____	_____
cars	_____	_____	_____
health	_____	_____	_____
accidents	_____	_____	_____
work	_____	_____	_____
hobbies	_____	_____	_____
the environment	_____	_____	_____
other people	_____	_____	_____
new friends	_____	_____	_____
learning language	_____	_____	_____

Check your answers with a partner.

Group work. Make a list of the things you talk about with your friends. Discuss them with another group. What are the three most popular topics?

Do you talk about different things with different people? Fill in the chart.

Family	Close Friends	School Friends/Co-workers

IN FOCUS
SOCIAL NETWORKS

The family is important in most societies. However, in Western societies family ties are often not as close as they are in non-Western societies. Some people rarely see their families, even when they live in the same city. Many young people prefer to spend their leisure time with their friends rather than their families.

How do people feel about family and friends in your country? How often do they see family and friends?

Review

1 🔈 **Listen and find Jean, Tina, and Amanda.**

🔈 **Listen again and write the key words that helped you.**

Jean _____

Tina _____

Amanda _____

2 **Circle the word that does not belong.**

a ▷	blond	tall	short	average height
b ▷	lazy	friendly	busy	serious
c ▷	slim	fat	tall	thin
d ▷	disappointed	boring	smart	interesting

87

3 Listen and circle the words you hear in Task 2.

 Listen again and fill in the chart.

Description	Occupation	Interest	Reason for doing course
Paula			
Bob			
Anna			

 Listen again. What language are they studying? Who do you think will be the most/least successful? Why?

4 Listen and circle the right answer for you.

a	Yes, I am.	Not really.
b	Yes, I would.	I don't think so.
c	Yes, I do.	No, I don't.

d	I guess I am.	No, not really.
e	Yes, I do.	No, I don't.

5 Look over the material in this book, and write down five questions you would like to ask your classmates. Make a survey.

Pair work. Survey another student.

Tell the class about your partner.